Dear Judy,

My love, and may these short lines give you comfort.

Aunt Lais

Words of Comfort and Hope

Illustrations by Otto Geipel

Words of Comfort And Hope

HALLMARK EDITIONS

What a new face

courage puts on everything!

RALPH WALDO
EMERSON

Concentrate on happy things
To keep your spirits high...
Think of things like tulips
Throwing kisses to the sky...
Think of cuddly kittens...
Children dancing in the hills...
And butterflies a-flutter
Over waking daffodils.

CHRIS FITZGERALD

I never knew a night so black
Light failed to follow on its track.
I never knew a storm so gray
It failed to have its clearing day.
I never knew such bleak despair
That there was not a rift, somewhere.
I never knew an hour so drear
Love could not fill it full of cheer!

JOHN KENDRICK BANGS

*T*here is a day of sunny rest
For every dark and troubled night:
And grief may hide an evening guest,
But joy shall come with early light.

WILLIAM CULLEN BRYANT

Tears are blessings, let them flow.

HARRY HUNTER

In the hour of adversity be not without hope
For crystal rain falls from black clouds.

NIZAMI (*Persian Poet*)

Oh, then indulge thy grief, nor fear to tell
The gentle source from whence thy sorrows flow!
Nor think it weakness when we love to feel,
Nor think it weakness what we feel to show.

WILLIAM COWPER

From the lowest depth

there is a path

to the loftiest height.

THOMAS CARLYLE

*M*usic is a delight because of its rhythm and flow. Yet the moment you arrest the flow and prolong a note or chord beyond its time, the rhythm is destroyed. Because life is likewise a flowing process, change and death are its necessary parts. To work for their exclusion is to work against life.

ALAN W. WATTS

May God give you that consolation which is beyond all earthly powers. ABRAHAM LINCOLN

Whenever evil befalls us, we ought to ask ourselves, after the first suffering, how we can turn it into good. So shall we take occasion, from one bitter root, to raise perhaps many flowers.

LEIGH HUNT

The soul would have no rainbow
Had the eyes no tears.

JOHN VANCE CHENEY

Walk on a rainbow trail;

NAVAJO SONG   walk on a trail of song,

and all about you will be beauty.

There is a way out of every dark mist,

over a rainbow trail.

At the onset of fear and alarm, or when trouble and stress are at hand, I will bless Him with special thanksgiving, and muse upon His power, and rely on His mercies always, and come thereby to know that in His hand lies the judgment of all living, and that all His words are truth.

From THE DEAD SEA SCRIPTURES

*Keep your face to the sunshine
and you cannot see the shadow.*

HELEN KELLER

Be perfect, be of good comfort, be of one mind, live in peace; and the God of love and peace shall be with you.

2 CORINTHIANS 13: 11

You have to believe in happiness,
   Or happiness never comes...
Oh, that's the reason a bird can sing —
On his darkest day he believes in Spring.

DOUGLAS MALLOCH

$\mathcal{D}$ifficulty is a severe instructor, set over us by the Supreme guardian and legislator, who knows us better than we know ourselves, and loves us better too. He that wrestles with us strengthens our nerves and sharpens our skill. Our antagonist is our helper.

EDMUND BURKE

Heaven knows we need never be ashamed of our tears, for they are rain upon the blinding dust of earth, overlying our hard hearts.

CHARLES DICKENS

One must have spiritual strength and remain brave and cheerful in these hard times. Pain and suffering are but externals; for such things it is not worth losing God's love and the ability to smile.

GUY DE LARIGAUDIE

Every dark night has a bright ending.

PERSIAN PROVERB

What sunshine is to flowers, smiles are to humanity.
They are but trifles to be sure; but, scattered along
life's pathway, the good they do is inconceivable.

JOSEPH ADDISON

*E*ven in the darkest hours of life let us remember with
comfort and assurance that for each of us something of
paradise is left: in the certainty of God's love, which
supports us, in the beauty of the stars and flowers and
in the happiness which radiates from a child's eyes.

NICODEMUS

And when the floods have spent themselves, the clouds part to let the blue sky tremble through them, and the west wind bears them away seaward, and, though they are yet black and threatening, we see their silver edges as they pass, and know that just behind them are singing birds and glittering dewdrops; and, lo! while yet we look, the sun bursts forth, and lights them up in the eastern heaven with the glory of the rainbow.

HENRY WARD BEECHER

The
Beautiful Promises
of God

God hath not promised skies always blue,
Flower-strewn pathways all our lives through.
God hath not promised sun without rain,
Joy without sorrow, peace without pain.

God hath not promised we shall not know
Toil and temptations, trouble and woe.
He hath not told us we shall not bear
Many a burden, many a care.
But God hath promised strength for the day,
Rest for the laborer, light for the way,
Grace for the trials, help from above,
Unfailing sympathy, undying love.

ANNIE JOHNSON FLINT

Thy sunshine smiles
upon the winter days of my heart,
never doubting   RABINDRANATH TAGORE
of its spring flowers.

We will grieve not, rather find
Strength in what remains behind….

WILLIAM WORDSWORTH

*H*ave courage for the great sorrows of life and patience
for the small ones. And when you have finished your
daily task, go to sleep in peace. God is awake.

VICTOR HUGO

Weeping may endure for a night,
but joy cometh   PSALM 30:5

in the morning.

Mirth is like a flash of lightning, that breaks through a gloom of clouds, and glitters for a moment; cheerfulness keeps up a kind of daylight in the mind, and fills it with a steady and perpetual serenity.

JOSEPH ADDISON

*W*hat life means to us is determined not so much by what life brings to us as by the attitude we bring to life; not so much by what happens to us as by our reaction to what happens.

LEWIS L. DUNNINGTON

Hast thou a grief? Go clasp it to thy breast;
Hast thou a poison? Drain it to the end.
Cry then, cry all thy heart out with its pain;
Hearts grow again, and eyes have better sight
After too many tears, as summer rain
Washes the air, and leaves it sweet and bright,
And birds step out on trees, whose happy song
Is often stilled, but never stilled for long.

ROBERT NATHAN
From "Autumn Sonnets #23"

God speaks sometimes through our circumstances and guides us, closing doors as well as opening them.

He will let you know what you must do, and what you must be. He is waiting for you to touch Him. The hand of faith is enough.

PETER MARSHALL

No soul is desolate as long as there is a human being for whom it can feel trust and reverence.

GEORGE ELIOT

Only one principle will give you courage; that is the principle that no evil lasts forever nor indeed for very long. EPICURUS

Sometimes I go about pitying myself, and all the time I am being carried on great winds across the sky.

AMERICAN INDIAN SAYING

I find the great thing in this world
is not so much where we stand,

as in what direction

we are moving.

OLIVER WENDELL HOLMES

*A*ll our progress is an unfolding, like the vegetable bud. You have first an instinct, then an opinion, then a knowledge, as the plant has root, bud, and fruit. Trust the instinct to the end, though you can render no reason.   RALPH WALDO EMERSON

Faith lifts up shining arms and points to a happier world where our loved ones await us.

HELEN KELLER

There is nothing in the world so much admired as a man who knows how to bear unhappiness with courage.

SENECA

*B*e willing to have it so. Acceptance of what has happened is the first step to overcoming the consequences of any misfortune.

WILLIAM JAMES

Troubles are often the tools by which God fashions us for better things.

HENRY WARD BEECHER

*W*hen the day returns, call us up with morning faces and with morning hearts, eager to labor, happy if happiness be our portion, and if the day be marked for sorrow, strong to endure.

ROBERT LOUIS STEVENSON

To know the rose
Is to know God,
To know the faded rose will bud again
Is to know Eternity.

LEWIS NICKERSON

In the garden of life, just think of the flowers
And pass the rest as you go;
Remember the bright and sunshiny hours
And forget the rain and the snow;
Think of the friends who are loyal and true,
Let the rest of the world go its way;
Remember the years but forget the tears,
And you'll find contentment each day!

EMILY R. GRAY

Like a bird singing in the rain,

let grateful memories

survive in time of sorrow.

ROBERT LOUIS STEVENSON

There is a law in life:
when one door closes to us
another one opens.

ANDRÉ GIDE

Sorrows are often like clouds, which though black
when they are passing over us, when they are past
become as if they were the garments of God, thrown
off in purple and gold along the sky.

HENRY WARD BEECHER

*W*here true serenity and boundless trust in God's
goodness prevail, man will not, in spite of cares, give
himself over to excessive pain. For we are certain that God
is always a wise and good father even when He sends
trials and tribulations.   NICODEMUS

We always hope; and in all things it is better to hope than to despair. When we return to real trust in God, there will no longer be room in our soul for fear.

JOHANN WOLFGANG VON GOETHE

There is no bond of grief so strong
but Love can give release…
no heartache so unbearable
but Love can bring you peace.

BARBARA BURROW

Our Creator would never have made such lovely
days and have given us the deep hearts to enjoy them,
above and beyond all thought, unless we were meant
to be immortal. NATHANIEL HAWTHORNE

Peace I leave with you, my peace I give unto you: not
as the world giveth, give I unto you. Let not your
heart be troubled, neither let it be afraid.

ST. JOHN 14: 27

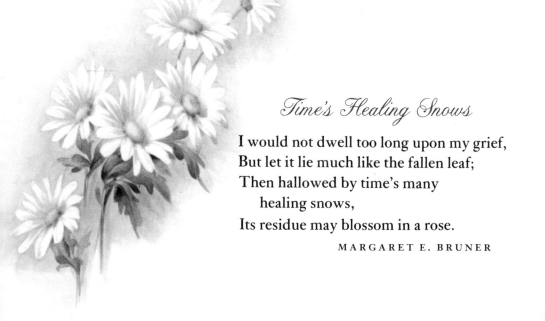

Time's Healing Snows

I would not dwell too long upon my grief,
But let it lie much like the fallen leaf;
Then hallowed by time's many
    healing snows,
Its residue may blossom in a rose.

MARGARET E. BRUNER

Just as there comes a warm sunbeam into every cottage window, so comes a love-beam of God's care and pity for every separate need.

NATHANIEL HAWTHORNE

Seek refuge in inner calm, free your thoughts from the external world and you will feel the rays of God's goodness and love pouring over you and the universe.

PERSIAN PROVERB

When you have shut your doors, and darkened your room, remember never to say that you are alone; for God is within and your genius is within, and what need have they of light to see what you are doing?

EPICTETUS

*N*othing happens to anybody which he is not fitted by nature to bear.

MARCUS AURELIUS

Sorrow knocked at the door,

Faith answered,

And found no one there.

JAPANESE PROVERB

This world is not conclusion;
A sequel stands beyond,
Invisible, as music,   EMILY DICKINSON
But positive, as sound.